W9-BGM-538

Ex-Library: Friends of
Lake County Public Library

ADVENTURERS

MOTOCROSS & TRIALS

Jeremy Evans

CRESTWOOD HOUSE

New York

LAKE COUNTY PUBLIC LIBRARY

First Crestwood House edition 1993

3 3113 01338 0391

© Julian Holland Publishing Ltd 1993

First published by Heinemann Library, 1993, an imprint of Heinemann Educational, a division of Heinemann Publishers (Oxford) Ltd, Halley Court, Jordan Hill, Oxford OX2 8EJ

All rights reserved. No part of this book may be reproduced or transmitted in any form or by any means, electronic or mechanical, including photocopying, recording, or by any information storage and retrieval system, without permission in writing from the Publisher.

Crestwood House
Macmillan Publishing Company
866 Third Avenue
New York, NY 10022

First edition

Macmillan Publishing Company is part of the Maxwell Communications Group of Companies.

Design by Julian Holland Publishing Ltd

Printed in Hong Kong

1 2 3 4 5 6 7 8 9 10

Library of Congress Cataloging-in-Publication Data
Evans, Jeremy.
    Motocross & Trials / by Jeremy Evans. — 1st ed.
      p. cm. — (Adventurers)
    Includes index.
    Summary: An introduction to off-road motorcycling, discussing choosing a bike, riding techniques, clothing, safety, and motocross racing.
    ISBN 0-89686-821-4
    1. Motorcycling—Juvenile literature. 2. Motocross—Juvenile literature. [1. Motorcycling. 2. Motocross.] I. Title.
    II. Series.
    GV1059.5.E93   1994
    796.7'56—dc20   93-9385

Acknowledgments
Illustrations: Rupert White Studio
Photographs: *a = above, b = below*
All photographs were taken by the author except:
Front cover, Kawasaki; title page, Kawasaki; 4a, Yamaha; 7a, Kawasaki; 7b, Kawasaki; 9a, Kawasaki; 11b, Kawasaki; 19a, Kawasaki; 21b, Kawasaki; 23b, Kawasaki; 24a, Kawasaki; 24b, Yamaha; 25, Kawasaki; 26a, Kawasaki; 27b, Kawasaki; 28b, Kawasaki; 29, Kawasaki; 33, Kawasaki; 34b, Eric Kitchen; 36b, Eric Kitchen; 37, Eric Kitchen; 38, Eric Kitchen; 39a, Eric Kitchen; 39b, Eric Kitchen; 43a, Eric Kitchen; 43b, Eric Kitchen; 45a, Eric Kitchen.

Thanks go to the Kawasaki Information Service and Mitsui Machinery Sales (Yamaha) for supplying motocross photos, and to Eric Kitchen for his peerless trials photos. Thanks also to the Portsmouth Schoolboy Scrambles Club, the Weymouth Beach Bash, and the Waterlooville Motorcycle Club's National Hoad Trophy Trial, whose events all contributed greatly to this book.

Thanks to Mike Rapley for his helpful comments on the manuscript.

Note to the reader
In this book there are some words in the text which are printed in **bold** type. This shows that the word is listed in the glossary on pages 46–47. The glossary gives a brief explanation of words that may be new to you.

Contents

Starting off-road

Great fun, but only in the right place at the right time

Knobby-tired bikes

This book is about **off-road motorcycles**. These are recognizable by their **knobby tires**, heavy-duty **suspension**, high **ground clearance** and tough appearance. In the hands of experts these bikes can go almost anywhere off-road. They can plow through deep mud, go up or down the steepest hills, tackle rocks and boulders and even forge a flooded river or stream. They can be used simply for the pleasure of exploring off-road trails or for competitions such as **motocross** and **trials**.

Trials

Organized competition is the best way to enjoy one of these off-road motorcycles. Learn how to ride it safely in places where you are allowed to ride.

Trials are popular worldwide. This is a competition in which the rider is matched against the terrain. He or she is required to ride along difficult sections that will tax riding skills to the limit. Balance and throttle control are what it is all about; speed is of minor importance. The top riders perform incredible feats, as they jump their bikes across huge boulders and up almost vertical cliffs.

Motocross

Motocross, or **MX**, is off-road motorcycle racing. It's about speed, skill and tactics. The riders race around tough, rough tracks, throwing mud or dust everywhere.

With bikes riding together at speed over difficult terrain, motocross is potentially much more dangerous than trials, but by careful planning, the organizers try to ensure accident-free events. Safety is particularly important for the youngest riders.

A motocross race is fast, noisy and closely fought.

Enduro and special events

Special events for off-road motorcycles range from **beach racing** (where a beach is transformed into a specially built racetrack) to long-distance on- and off-road marathons known as **enduros,** which cover many hundreds of miles and require navigational as well as riding skills. The longest enduros are the classic **marathons**, such as the Paris to Dakar Race, in which specially prepared cars and motorcycles race across the continent of Africa.

Getting sand in your face! Beach racing entertains both racers and spectators.

5

The parts of a bike

throttle/brake

twin front
suspension shock
absorbers

clutch

liquid cooling

monoshock rear suspension

exhaust

swinging arm

front disc brake

rear disc brake

All off-road bikes can be stripped to
this stage quickly and easily for
maintenance and cleaning.

Trials or motocross?

The motocross bike needs power and
straight-line performance, together with
good handling around the racetrack. The
trials bike must have perfect balance, superb
lightweight handling and phenomenal hill-
climbing ability. You can tell the two
machines apart at a glance. While a
motocross bike looks mean and powerful, a
trials bike is smaller and lighter, with a
shorter **wheelbase** and higher ground
clearance, and the **crankcase** protected by
its all-important **skid plate**.

(Right) A trials bike needs perfect balance.

Frame and suspension

An off-road motorcycle is built around its **frame**. Made of thin-wall, large diameter steel tubing, the frame must be as light and as rigid as possible. The frame geometry must be designed to accommodate the engine and all the fittings that make up the bike, including a rear subframe at the back. The **center of gravity** must be kept directly under the rider for balance and ease of handling.

Suspension is very important. The front and rear suspension need up to 11 inches of travel. This is provided by two hydraulic forks for the front wheel and **monoshock suspension** for the back wheel.

A powerful rear suspension unit for MX

A wide-diameter disc brake combined with "upside-down" front forks

Brakes, tires and wheels

Efficient braking is as important as engine performance. On an off-road motorcycle there should be **front** and **rear disc brakes** for powerful, progressive braking. Use of the lightest possible wheels reduces the unsprung weight of the bike and improves its traction.

The standard tires provided on a trials or MX bike are designed to perform well in all conditions. However, an expert competing at top level may choose from a dozen or more different tread patterns and rubber compounds. Even then a tire that's suitable for one part of the course may not be so good on another.

The engine

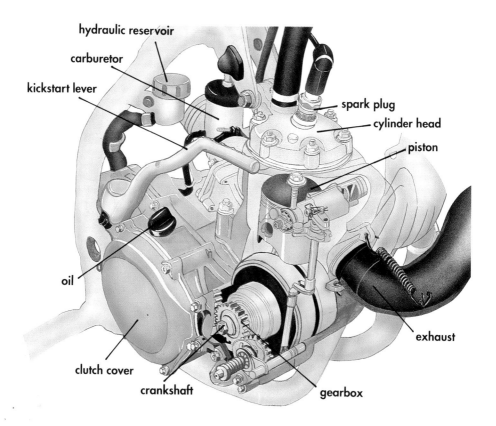

hydraulic reservoir

carburetor

kickstart lever

spark plug

cylinder head

piston

oil

clutch cover

crankshaft

gearbox

exhaust

An engine for off-road use must deliver strong, efficient, reliable power under the most difficult conditions, and still be easy to clean and to work on. It must also be a lightweight, compact unit.

Most bikes used for trials and motocross have a single-cylinder, **liquid-cooled,** two-stroke engine. For motocross use, engines start with the 51cc size used for the schools' Junior Class. Bigger sizes of engine cater to heavier and more experienced riders, with a choice of 80cc and 100cc sharing the same frame size, and 125cc usually in a bigger frame. Then there is a big jump in performance to the 250cc engines delivering over 50 horsepower. Most powerful of all is the 500cc Grand Prix class engine, which delivers around 65hp.

Engines for trials require short spurts of power to get them up and over seemingly impossible obstacles. The favorite size is usually around 250cc, which delivers sufficient power while remaining light and compact enough for the bike to be handled easily.

Engine choice

Choosing the right engine partly depends on how big and strong the rider is. In motocross a smaller engine has to **rev** higher than a larger engine to keep up with it. A 125cc bike may go very fast, but the constant use of high revs most of the way around the track puts a lot of wear and tear on the engine and means that the rider needs to keep it going flat out to make the most of its potential.

A 250cc engine may be more powerful than a 125cc by some 15hp, but is heavier, and the bike it powers may be no faster around the track. However, a 250cc bike is likely to be easier to ride fast and in the long term is probably cheaper to maintain.

A 500cc motocross engine is extremely fast and only for experts.

Why two-stroke?

Most motocross and trials bikes have **two-stroke** engines. These provide the right combination of light weight and power for smaller engines — under about 300cc —for off-road use. They are also easier to maintain than four-stroke engines.

The spark plug of a two-stroke engine ignites the gas on alternate upward strokes of the piston. This is called the **power stroke**. It pushes the piston and connecting rod down, turning the crankshaft, which drives the back wheel via the gearbox and chain.

Safety first

● Read the owner's manual for your machine thoroughly.
● Keep yourself and your machine in good condition.
● Wear protective clothing — helmet, goggles and boots.
● Never carry a passenger.
● Take it easy and don't overextend yourself.
● Ride safely, respect other riders and take care of the environment.
● Be sure your machine is suitable for both on-road and off-road use.

Buying a bike

The first choice is, do you want a bike for trials, motocross or just enjoying off-road trails? As an off-road sport, motocross has the advantage of having classes and sizes of bikes for all ages of rider from six years old up, but the bikes are usually not legal on the road. Trials tend to attract the older rider, especially because the sections in an event may be joined by on-road riding. This requires a motorcycle endorsement and a bike that is legal. So does any trials riding that takes place on highways.

(Above) The Gas-Gas, a successful trials bike from Spain
(Left) The 125cc size range is a popular choice for teenage motocross riders and extremely fast. Note the massive back wheel clearance, which allows for suspension movement and ground clearance.

Which brand?

Kawasaki is a popular choice in the 60cc MX class.

The choice of bikes for motocross is dominated by the big Japanese motorcycle manufacturers, such as Kawasaki, Honda, Suzuki and Yamaha. In trials the choice is much wider, with several small, specialized manufacturers producing world-class bikes that can take on the Japanese giants. Many are built in Spain and Italy, such as Gas-Gas, Aprilia, Montesa and Beta.

New or secondhand?

Buying a new bike is obviously more expensive than buying secondhand. However, if the dealer is an expert in motocross or trials, you will get the best advice and after-sales backup.

There is always a wide choice of secondhand machines, since riders near the top like to change their bikes fairly often. If you opt to go secondhand:
● Buy the best bike you can afford.
● Get expert advice.
● Buy only a completely safe bike.
● Allow for the cost of servicing and accessories.
● Never buy a bike in poor condition.

Top riders get new bikes each season but use them hard.

11

Clothing

A motocross rider needs to be fully protected front and back.

Helmets and boots

Never ride without a **helmet**. The helmet should satisfy road safety standards and must be a close and comfortable fit. With the helmet you will need scratch-resistant **goggles**. Some have **tear-offs** to enable you to see clearly in muddy conditions.

Boots should be flexible, strong and close fitting. They should have strong shin protection, with a sole that allows them to skate over the ground while riding, and enough grip to enable you to walk or push the bike if required.

Body protection

Body armor for motocross is made of lightweight plastic with foam lining. It helps protect the upper body — in particular, collarbones, shoulders, upper arms and spine — but is not worn for trials.

Gloves should offer total finger protection, with a curved palm that fits comfortably on the controls. A rider will need different pairs for riding in summer and winter. Specially designed pants for motocross or trials are made from fully washable synthetic materials, sometimes with leather seats for comfort and durability.

Dressed for motocross. Note the extra knee and upper body protection and the heavy-duty boots. A waterproof suit keeps off the worst of the mud in wet conditions.

13

Upkeep and accessories

A power hose is a useful accessory, but one that needs a light touch.

Washing the bike

An off-road bike should always be kept clean of mud and dirt.
A high-pressure hose works quickly but can be harmful. Some are so powerful that they will force water into sealed parts of the bike and even blast off the paint. Once water gets in, there is no way of getting it out without a major rebuild.

An ordinary hose does the job more slowly but is just as effective when used with a stick to push off clinging mud. A small brush is useful to clean the wheel spokes.

Drying and checking

After it is washed, the bike should be laid on its side so that any water can drain away. Starting the engine should blow out and evaporate any remaining water.

Follow the handbook's instructions for routine lubrication and maintenance. Check the oil seals for leakage, and examine the tires for wear. All nuts, screws and other fittings should be checked for tightness. Finally, you should touch up chipped paint and polish the whole bike.

The toolkit

A complete **toolkit** for maintaining an off-road motorcycle is expensive. If you plan to do all your own maintenance, you will need the following tools:
- Ring wrenches $^5/_{16}$ to $^{15}/_{16}$ inches
- Open-end wrenches $^5/_{16}$ to $^{15}/_{16}$ inches
- Socket set
- Torque wrench
- Regular screwdrivers
- Phillips screwdrivers
- Hammer
- Allen wrenches
- Tire pressure gauge
- Tire pump and tire levers
- Various spares such as chain links, spark plugs, nuts and bolts, rags, etc.
- A clean container to hold anything removed from the bike.

With this kind of use, your bike needs a lot of care.

Safety first

- Brake fluid absorbs water, which interferes with the brake action. The fluid should be replaced regularly.
- Check the brake and **throttle** cables frequently.
- Avoid breathing in vapor from cleaners.
- Gas and gas vapor are highly explosive. Keep all flames away.
- Oil damages the environment. Avoid spills.

Keeping the bike running is part of the fun!

15

Riding trails

Off-road riding is fun, but don't annoy other countryside users.

Where to go

Other people will not necessarily appreciate the noise of your motorcycle as you have a great time riding off-road in the countryside. It is imperative to go only where it is legal to ride. Even then you should take great care not to upset other countryside users. Unfortunately the choice for motorcycles in most areas is likely to be pretty limited, as most tracks and trails are open only to walkers and sometimes horseback riders or mountain bikers. If you're determined to go it alone, finding places to ride off-road is never easy. The best way to find information on where to ride is to join a club.

Joining a club

Most countries where off-road motorcycling is popular have various local clubs to join. They are usually well organized and give you the chance to meet people, exchange information, get help sorting out problems with your bike and go riding together. Most clubs concentrate on organized competition such as trials or motocross "scrambles." If that doesn't appeal to you, they should be able to provide information on where you can and cannot go. For a start, contact one of the organizations listed on page 46 to get details of clubs in your area.

Considering others

● Make sure you ride only where and when it is legal to do so.
● Slow down for mountain bikes.
● Slow down and always give way to walkers and horseback riders.
● Slow down for dogs and when passing all farm animals.
● Ride carefully. Don't rip up the trail.
● Respect the countryside. Aim to make the minimum impact on your surroundings.

Heading off with the family on a "green road."

Be safe – never ride off-road alone!

Safety first

● Prepare your route carefully.
● Carry a map.
● Tell someone where you are going and when you expect to be back.
● Don't get caught off-road at nightfall.
● Never ride on the road at night without lights.
● Ride in company. Three is a good number for safety and fun.
● Always wear a helmet and full protective gear.
● Make sure you have suitable clothing, particularly if you are riding in high hills.

Motocross

Countdown to the start of a race at a motocross meeting

What it's about

Motocross originated in Britain. After the pioneering Scott Trials in 1914 — a classic trials event that is still held in England — some motorcycle enthusiasts organized the first official off-road "scrambles" at Camberley Heath in 1924.

The sport was originally known as scrambling but changed its name to motocross, or MX, with world championship events in the 1950s. The sport is now international at all levels. Racing is usually held on a course about a mile and a quarter long, with plenty of hills, bumps and bends to test riders and bikes to the limit.

When to start

There are classes for youth motocross riders from 7 years of age to 17. Young riders start with the smallest 51cc "automatic" bikes, moving up through the 80cc, 100cc, and 125cc classes as they get older. In some countries the authorities advocate not starting until you're at least 15 years old, as it's a tough sport both physically and mentally. Elsewhere, the 51cc class often has the biggest starting line at junior meetings. As the riders get older and move up through the classes, the competition gets tougher and more expensive and racers begin to drop out.

Action in the superfast 500cc Grand Prix class is for experts only.

Preparing to ride

A motocross bike has the same basic controls as a road bike, but there the similarities end. Before taking part in a race, you should learn to handle and ride the bike in all conditions. You will need to master the basics of accelerating, braking and cornering on a rough or muddy surface. The first requirement is to find somewhere to practice. Be sure you have permission to do so, and don't practice alone; you'll want help if you fall off and hurt yourself. The basic riding position is standing on the foot **pegs**, with your feet pointing down and your arms straight. Get used to this position, and make sure the foot controls for rear brake and gearshift are correct. Adjust them if necessary. Then start riding. Try moving your weight over the front and back wheels to discover the huge difference weight distribution makes in the handling of a highly responsive motocross bike.

Race preparation

First, make sure you have all the tools for regular maintenance, plus a selection of spare parts. Check your clothing and safety gear, and in cold conditions take extra warm clothing for when you're not racing. Get to the race in plenty of time to have your bike checked by the tech inspectors, and sign with the organizers to confirm your entry. If possible, walk around the track before racing starts, to decide how you will ride it.

The mechanical-gate starting system drops flat to let the riders get away.

The start

It is vital to get a good start. Motocross races are usually of short duration, and it is much easier to be in front from the beginning. The riders behind are blinded by the mud and dust thrown up by the leader and have the problem of finding a "line" to overtake. In the final seconds before the start, the riders open their throttles to give peak **torque**. As the starting gate goes down or the line goes up, the rider eases in the clutch, getting away as fast as possible without too much wheelspin. Weight position is critical. If your weight is too far back, the bike may flip over on its back wheel. However, if your weight is too far forward, the back wheel will spin without driving the bike.

Seconds after the start, the leaders are already well ahead of the field.

Controlling wheelies

For straight-line riding, a motocross bike is perfectly balanced when its front wheel is just starting to lift off the ground. The **wheelie** is caused by the immense power of the back wheel and is controlled by using the throttle and body weight together. If you lean your weight over the back wheel, you get maximum drive, but the front wheel will lift uncontrollably high. You must lean forward and backward to control this until the bike is balanced. Most of a motocross race is ridden standing. Controlling a wheelie when sitting is more difficult, since you can't move your weight as effectively. It relies on precise throttle control.

Lean forward and backward or lose control!

Choosing a line

A good time to overtake is in the crowd at the first turn.

The **racing line** is the fastest line around a track. It will vary from rider to rider, according to their expertise in tackling difficult sections. Equally important is a **passing line,** which enables you to overtake the rider in front. The racing line sets up the rider to tackle the next turn or straight at top speed; the passing line is the fastest line through a small section of the course which enables you to overtake. For instance, if the racing line follows the outside of the turn, the passing line might cut across the turn on the inside. This line will slow you down for the next section but will get you through the turn fast enough to overtake the racer who follows the racing line and is then stuck behind you.

When to brake

An expert rider accelerates or brakes all the way around the track. When you are braking for a turn, timing is critical. The technique is to brake going into the turn, keeping the brake on until you can power out of the turn. If you hit the brakes and then have to accelerate going into the turn, you have braked too early and deserve to get overtaken. It is important to brake and accelerate smoothly. Hard braking and hitting a bump can result in a **tank slapper,** when the back wheel kicks up into the air. This is corrected by opening the throttle to drive the back wheel down.

How to brake

The front hand brake slows the bike and is usually controlled by two fingers; the rear foot brake keeps the bike on line. Braking drives the front forks down, so the rider must move his or her weight back on the bike to keep control of the front wheel. If the front wheel locks and starts to slide when braking, the rider eases off the brakes to keep the bike straight.

Two fingers control braking into the turn.

Bumps and whoops

The front suspension soaks up the bumps.

The technique for riding over bumps is to allow the front forks to rise up and down their full length to absorb the impact. The rider stands with weight well back and power full on to maintain control, shifting down a gear to have enough revs to accelerate out of each bump.

Whoops are a series of closely spaced bumps. The trick is to keep the front wheel high enough off the ground to go over the top of each whoop – but no higher, or the bike loses control and speed. A burst of throttle control is used to lift the front wheel just before it hits each whoop, while powering the back wheel over.

23

Power slides

Moving your weight forward so that the gas tank is between your legs allows the front wheel to take over as the wheel that's controlling the bike. This can be used to **power slide** a bike, the fastest way to change direction to get around a turn and accelerate onto the next straight in dry conditions. The rider slows for the curve, shifts down to a low gear and brings the weight forward. With no weight over the back wheel, opening the throttle makes the bike slide out away from the turn. To correct this and prevent falling, the rider instantly turns the front wheel in the direction of the slide away from the turn. The amount of back wheel slide is controlled by the throttle, with the inside boot sometimes being held out to help balance.

Power sliding a 500cc bike with both feet and power on

The fastest way to corner in dry conditions if the turn is wide enough to slide

Berm bashing

A **berm** is a banked wall of earth on the outside of a curve, which in wet conditions is piled up and pushed out by the action of passing riders. Riding around the berm is often the racing line for the leaders, using a technique called **berm bashing**. The basic technique is to hit the berm hard, keeping weight over the front wheel to stay on the berm rather than go over the top as the rider accelerates out of the curve.

Riding on the loose earth of the berm absorbs a lot of power, but this is balanced by the fact that berm bashers can leave their braking until very late. Advanced riders compensate for the power loss by hitting berms about halfway around, power sliding through the first part of the curve and sitting down on the bike as it hits the berm. The inside leg is held out to keep the bike up if it slides out too far.

Kawasaki factory team rider Paul Malin power slides into the berm, with his inside leg held out to balance the bike.

Uphills

World champion Dave Thorpe hits the top of the hill at the British GP.

When powering uphill, the front wheel becomes very light, and the rider must keep weight well forward over the handlebars to press it down and prevent a backward loop. Easing off the throttle slows the bike quickly and brings the front wheel down but carries the risk of stalling and stopping. Selecting a gear that allows plenty of power is important to keep the bike moving fast, slipping the clutch if necessary. Forward weight must be balanced with rear wheel traction, especially if the surface is soft mud. One technique is to allow wheelspin all the way up the hill to prevent the rear tire from becoming clogged.

Safety first

Before the race:
- Check your tires.
- Check your brakes.
- Check your gas level.
- Check for anything missing or coming loose on the bike.
- Check your helmet is secure.
- Check your goggles are clean and unscratched.
- Check your boots are on correctly.
- Check your body armor.
- Learn the course and work out racing and passing lines.

Downhills

Racers find the fastest downhill line on a very muddy track.

Weight distribution and throttle control are critical on downhills. The rider's weight must be kept back to lighten the load on the front suspension, with arms slightly bent to help absorb bumps and lumps. To keep the back wheel down, it's often necessary to keep power on, while shifting through the gears to help control speed. Braking on hills requires extra care. If the suspension is pushed down by braking and riding downhill, it won't get around a curve easily. The technique is to brake before the turn so you can then accelerate into the curve. This will lift the front suspension and make the turn easier to negotiate.

Keeping power on helps keep the back wheel from lifting.

27

Jumping

Hit the smallest bump fast enough, and a motocross bike will become airborne. Launch off a good-size hill, and the jump can be over 25 yards! The technique is to select the right gear to enable you to jump with the power on. If a bike is jumped with the power off, it will flop down to the ground out of control.

The rider shifts body weight back and accelerates into takeoff, lifting the front wheel into a wheelie with the back wheel taking off behind. The throttle is closed immediately on takeoff, with the front wheel kept higher than the back for a safe rear wheel landing. The braking effect of the back wheel drops the front wheel back down onto the ground, with the rider absorbing the landing impact with the legs, sitting down and accelerating away.

The front wheel is kept up for a rear wheel landing.

Kicking out into a front wheel downhill landing is for experts only!

Jumping on hills

Jumping on hills requires better control. If you accelerate too hard going into an uphill jump, the wheelie may go too high and flip the bike over. It's vital for the rider to have his or her weight forward to keep the front wheel down on takeoff, and to hold it down when the bike lands on its back wheel.

For downhill jumps, the rider's weight needs to be brought back to the normal riding position for flat ground. As the bike takes off, it will fall away from the rider into the correct front-wheel-up position. When the bike lands on the back wheel, the front wheel will come down very heavily, and the rider has to accelerate hard immediately to push the back of the bike down and the front up.

A fully powered downhill jump with a 500 needs perfect technique.

Tactics

Psyching out

Overtaking relies on technique, tactics and psyching out the rider in front. The same is true of protecting your position from a rider behind. Attempts to overtake can result in a collision; invariably the bike that collides with its front wheel is the one that stalls or crashes, while the other rider carries on unscathed. This can lead to a number of "dirty tricks." For instance, if a rider is close behind another in a muddy rut, the front rider suddenly dips the clutch and brakes so the rider behind rides straight into the back wheel. A variation is for a rider who is being overtaken to give a burst on the throttle, sliding the back wheel out so that it hits the overtaking bike. Tricks like this are not pleasant, but as in many sports they do happen.

When you are aware of a competitor breathing down your neck, it takes experience not to become flustered. The rider behind may exploit this. If a fast rider is lapping the field, it is acceptable to shout and warn slower riders to pull over.

Showing a wheel, which is pushing your wheel into the line of vision of the rider in front even when you can't overtake, can be unsettling enough for the leading rider to make a mistake and let you by. A variation is to keep showing a wheel on one side, and then overtake on the other where the rider is not expecting you. However, if you get too close when showing a wheel, the rider in front may be able to cut across and knock you off.

Don't look back! It's easy to get psyched out with a rider just behind.

Motocross dangers and injuries

Falls in motocross racing are frequent, but injuries are surprisingly rare.

With a pack of bikes racing around a slippery track as fast as they can go, there is an element of danger in motocross. Injuries sometimes do occur but are generally much less severe than those in road racing. They are usually the result of falling off your bike and hitting something hard, getting hit by another rider or catching your foot in a rut. This may cause bruising, strained ligaments, dislocations or at worst fractured bones. In the event of a crash, experts advise rolling yourself into a ball with knees tucked into your chest, arms wrapped around your head to help protect it and avoid whiplash, and elbows pressed against your chest to protect the rib cage. When you hit the ground, coming to a sudden stop is what causes injury, so try to roll or slide out of trouble. Above all, ride carefully and sensibly, never put yourself or another rider in danger and always wear full protective gear.

Your signaler lets you know the score.

Safety and signals

Top riders out to win are often supported by a **signaler** who provides vital information about the rider's position: whether the rider is gaining on those in front, whether those behind are catching up, and how many laps there are to go. The signaler must display this information clearly, at an easy, straight part of the track where the rider is going slow enough to read it.

31

Sand racing

Racing on sand is not easy! The bikes dig deep ruts and throw up flying sand.

Beach events

Beach races are unique events in which a vacation beach can be transformed into a demanding course for motocross bikes. The races usually take place at popular seaside resorts out of the main summer season but close enough to the warm weather to guarantee a huge turnout. The beach is bulldozed into a course in a matter of hours, with straights, chicanes, twists, turns and artificial hills that change shape and flatten out as the races progress. The entry for these events is always large, despite the fact that sand is difficult to race on and smothers the bikes.

Beach technique

Most beach races are held on soft sand. It is vital to keep weight over the back wheel, keeping the front wheel light so it does not become buried in the sand and stall the bike. Smooth acceleration is important to prevent wheelspin, which would quickly dig the back wheel into a hole. From the start, the rider in front has a tremendous advantage as the sand gets churned up behind. Conditions are at their worst at the back of the field. Soft artificial sand hills may need to be climbed diagonally rather than straight on, with the power kept full on to avoid getting bogged down.

Supercross and marathons

Enduro

- **Supercross** takes place in a stadium and is often held indoors as an evening event. The racers use an artificially constructed earth track. Famous events include the Mickey Thompson Anaheim Supercross in California, which attracts 60,000 spectators.
- Marathon races are held over long distances off-road. Competitors often compete in different classes against four-wheel-drive vehicles, using special heavy-duty off-road bikes with extra fuel capacity.

Reliability enduro is a long-distance off-road race, usually lasting from one to six days, with off-road stages of 20 miles and more. Riders set off one at a time or in small groups and are allowed a time for each stage. The riders have no chance to check out the course before the event. They must be able to navigate and be capable of repairing the bike. Enduro bikes are supposed to be road legal, with lights and speedometers, and are usually heavier and more forgiving to ride than motocross bikes.

Enduro action during the Welsh Two-Day event, which follows forest tracks

Trials

Lining up for the start of a trials event. Riders leave at one-minute intervals.

Trials events

Trials is about technique, not speed. It is probably the oldest form of motorcycle competition. The first world-famous Scottish Six-Day Trials took place in 1909 when manufacturers used it to show off the capabilities of their bikes on the rough roads of those days.

Trials grew into an international sport, with events ranging from club meetings to a World Championship series. The terrain the riders are now asked to tackle is incredibly demanding, and the techniques and bikes used for trials have reached a high degree of sophistication.

Modern Scottish Six-Day action

Observed sections

A trials event is divided into **stages** containing **observed sections**. There may be six stages connected by road in a daylong event, with 40 or more sections in all. Each section may be no longer than 100 yards or even less and will have been marked out by an expert who ensures it is ridable. The competitors usually walk the section first to gauge its difficulties and then ride it one at a time.

A rider tackles a hillside section while an observer looks on.

Scoring

Each section is managed by an observer, who awards penalty points. The course is usually marked by blue and red flags; the rider must pass blue on the left and red on the right. If the rider completes the section without putting a foot down, it's a "clean" ride. Penalty points are awarded for **footing** or **dabbing**. The rider with the lowest score at the end of the event wins.

Handling a trials bike

No other motorcycle could climb like this.

A unique machine

A trials bike is like no other motorcycle. It is the most beautifully balanced machine with featherlight handling, which can be danced on the spot. It has a powerful engine — generally a single-cylinder two-stroke of around 250cc — with huge amounts of torque. But its six-speed gearbox offers a choice of such low gears that the bike can be ridden with power on at less than walking pace.

First practice

The riding position for a trials section is always standing up on the pegs. The legs should be kept virtually straight with knees well back.

Practice riding in tight circles, blipping the throttle to maintain control. When the bike can almost be turned in its own length, try balancing with a 45-degree half lock on the steering.

A wheelie is held under perfect control.

36

Improving balance

Jordi Tarres, Spanish world champion for Beta in 1991, shows incredible balance.

The technique for controlling the bike's speed when moving very slowly is to hold the brake and slip the clutch to ease power. This becomes more difficult in slippery conditions when the back wheel spins and slides. To practice, set a course between a straight line of markers about 3 feet apart. Learn to steer from lock to lock around these markers, steering so that the back wheel clears them as well. When you can steer through them without dabbing a foot, move the markers closer together and try again, stopping in the middle of the course to stand on the pegs with the bike stationary for as long as you can.

Wheelies

A trials bike wheelie can be lifted to 45 degrees or higher and held there by balance and throttle control, while the rider prepares to clear an obstacle like a big rock or fallen tree. The basic wheelie can be learned at walking speed. Ride along in second gear, close the throttle to dip the front suspension and on the rebound open the throttle to lift the front wheel. Close the throttle as soon as the front wheel is high enough.

37

Trials on rock

An aggressive attitude is necessary to get up rock climbs like this.

Difficulties and dangers

Rock comes in all shapes and sizes: loose stones or big, firm slabs; slimy, slithery rock; jagged edges with drops or holes in between. To overcome these obstacles, a rider should be confident and determined – not anxious about falling off. Although injuries do occur, they are rarely serious in competitions. However, it is important to wear full protective gear and *never* to practice alone. Rock is the toughest terrain that a trials bike has to handle. Soft suspension is necessary to avoid bouncing off the rocks. Climbing at high speed in a high gear is the way to cope with loose rock under the wheels.

Streams and slime

Streams with rock beds are a popular choice for observed sections. The trials expert will first walk the section, testing depth of water with a stick, looking out for loose rocks and checking for grip. The principal technique is to use more speed if the rocks are slippery, keeping the bike straight and riding over everything. Turning to avoid rocks often leads to dabbing a foot. Slime is very difficult to ride on. Late arrivals at a section may be lucky if the wheels and boots of previous riders have scrubbed the slime clear.

Loose rock and slime make riding treacherous.

The big drop! It's vital to know what's below.

Deep water

If a section is through hub-deep water, the rider must first wade through it to check for grip on the bottom, as well as looking out for underwater drops, rocks and other hazards. Deep water should generally be ridden at a high enough speed to get the bike past any other unexpected hazards, but not so fast that the wave pushed up by the front wheel drowns the engine. At the end of the section, the brakes must be dried. This can be done by applying light pressure and allowing them to heat up while riding.

39

Trials on mud

Mud, glorious mud! A few enthusiasts compete two-up with trials sidecars.

Riding on mud is the opposite of riding on rock; it's soft, but equally treacherous. Lack of grip is the obvious problem, and riders must check muddy sections carefully while observing the difficulties other riders experience. The principal technique is to keep the bike straight and moving in a high gear, with the bike kept upright to get maximum traction from the back tire. If the section has wet mud on one side and drier mud on the other, the wet mud may prove easier to ride through with the back wheel biting on the hard surface beneath. If the bike stops moving, one answer is to open the throttle wide and attempt to "burn" through the mud. This may result in a spectacular dismount! If you have to dab to maintain control, using three hard dabs to keep moving is better than failing to make it to the end of the section.

40

Trials in the woods

Sections that weave between trees demand tight turns from lock to lock, a technique known as **nadgery**. The handlebars must be gripped tightly, with just two fingers controlling the clutch and front brake. Sometimes the turns required are too tight for the bike to be steered around, and a rider uses the rear wheel pirouette. The front wheel is lifted into a wheelie, and the rider leans back and into the turn to pirouette the bike on its back wheel. When the bike is pointing in the correct direction, the rider leans forward to drop the front wheel.

Note the look of anticipation! A pirouette is the only answer for such a tight turn.

Root difficulties

Tree roots can be dangerously slippery and radiate at all angles on the ground. They are best tackled straight-on at a good speed in a high gear. If you hit a slippery tree root at an angle, one or both wheels will slide off. The front-wheel or two-wheel wheelie is needed to float the bike across. If you dab at a passing tree with your hand to maintain balance, you lose a point just as you would dabbing the ground.

Halfway through a woodland section, this rider pauses in perfect balance.

41

Steep uphills

There's no time for gear shifting on a steep uphill. You must get it right at the start.

Body weight and control

Uphill sections should be approached at full power, which will carry you to the top without shifting gears. If there isn't enough speed and power at the bottom of the section, using too much throttle or shifting gears on the hill is likely to cause wheelspin and lift the front wheel so you cannot steer. Keep your body vertical as the bike angles up the hill. Leaning forward will spin the back wheel, and leaning back may lead to a loop.

Dropping the bike

If you stall or lose control, don't dip the clutch — the bike will roll back down the hill. Instead, lay the bike down with the tires on the downward side. Keep holding the handlebars and consider where to go next.

Climbing rock steps

Climbing rock steps is one of trials' more amazing techniques. A wheelie lifts the front wheel up onto the top of the rock, and from there the rider powers up almost vertically on the back wheel with the bike in perfect balance.

An even more spectacular technique is the two-wheel wheelie. At the moment when the front wheel is about to drop down on the top of the step, the rider's weight is thrown onto the front of the bike. This lifts the back wheel, allowing the rider to guide the back of the bike up onto the step at the same time as the front wheel goes down.

Front wheel up, then power up on the back.

Ahvala flies the 183-pound Aprilia uphill.

Jumping uphill

Some sections in top competition call for daring techniques. If the rider is climbing rocks and there's a big drop in between, the only thing left may be to jump the gap. Such obstacles have to be tackled in full-on style, and a rider who backs off just won't make it. A master of the technique is 1992 world champion Tommi Ahvala, seen here launching uphill with the appropriately named Aprilia Climber, ready to land on the next rock on his unstoppable way uphill.

Steep downhills

A rider starts a long, slithery downhill on a chalk gully.

Confidence and control

To slow up the bike on a downhill, throttle back. Brake carefully but never slip the clutch, which would send the bike out of control. On a severely steep hill, drive the bike against the brakes, with the back brake fully locked to drag the back wheel. The clutch must be slipped to avoid stalling, with the throttle opened when it is necessary to clear the engine and keep it running smoothly. All the weight of the descent will be pushed onto the front wheel. To keep steering, pull the front brake on and off every few seconds, letting it off just before the front wheel locks and skids.

Descending rock steps

Some sections feature vertical drops or "steps," which are suitable only for experienced riders with plenty of nerve. The technique is to get weight back on the bike with arms held straight and rigid, as the bike drops over the edge and lands on its front wheel with the front suspension and rider's legs absorbing the shock. If the drop is longer than the length of the bike, the rider has to jump it down. The rider approaches the edge slowly, then gives a burst of acceleration to push the back wheel clear.

Rock steps can be pretty intimidating!

The observer is the backbone of the sport.

Signing off

At the end of each section the observer marks the rider's score. Marks are based on the official wording: "Dabbing will be considered to have occurred if any part of the body touches the ground or leans on an obstacle without stopping the progress of the machine." Observers are usually volunteers who spend the whole day marking riders, and are willing to stay out in wind, rain or sun. There may occasionally be disagreements over their marking, but most riders would agree that trials is a "sport" and protests should be avoided except at national and international level championship events.

International associations

The Auto-Cycle Union
Wood Street, Rugby,
Warwickshire CV21 2YX, UK

Automobile Association of
  South Africa
PO Box 596, Johannesburg 2000,
South Africa

Motorcycling Australia
3/10 Hoddle Street, PO Box 142
Abbotsford, Victoria 3067, Australia

Canadian Motorcycle Association
Box 448, Station B
Hamilton, Ontario L8L 8C4
Canada

American Motorcyclist Association
PO Box 6114
Westerville, Ohio 43081–6114

New Zealand Auto-Cycle Union
PO Box 253, Huntly 2191
New Zealand

Glossary

beach races: "sand racing" is a type of speedway held on a flat, oval course on sand, with artificial humps and bumps
berm: banked turn on a motocross course
berm bashing: hitting the berm to get the bike around the turn
body armor: plastic shields worn to protect the upper body and shoulders
boots: the best are heavy-duty leather with steel toe caps. MX boots should have smooth soles with no heels; trials boots should have heavily patterned heels and soles for maximum grip
brake: front brake is hand operated; back brake is foot operated
carburetor: mixes fuel and air as fuel goes into the cylinder
center of gravity: the point of balance on an off-road bike
clutch: engages and disengages the engine from the gears
crankcase: encloses the crankshaft
dabbing: putting down a foot in trials
enduro: a long-distance off-road event
exhaust: removes burned gases from cylinder
expansion chamber: part of the two-

stroke exhaust system that controls expansion of engine gases
footing: see **dabbing**
frame: the steel chassis on which the bike is built. Some trials bikes have aluminum frames
front disc brake: disc brakes use hydraulically operated pads that close on a metal disc to slow the wheel
front suspension shock absorbers: metal springs inside oil-filled tubes
goggles: full eye protection, which is vital for motocross
ground clearance: the distance between the lowest part of the frame and the ground
helmet: a thick, shock-absorbing inner liner made of foam with a hard outer skin of plastic, fiberglass, carbon fiber or Kevlar; modern designs should protect the chin, mouth and nose
knobby tires: tires with big, square rubber knobs to grip on off-road surfaces. The depth of tread used on trials bikes is restricted
liquid-cooled engine: most modern off-road bikes have liquid-cooled engines, with the coolant supplied from the

radiator

marathons: nonstop long-distance events

monoshock rear suspension: a lightweight suspension system with a single heavy-duty metal spring and oil-filled shock-absorbing tube

motocross: off-road motorcycle racing

MX: shorthand for motocross

nadgery: weaving around tight trees and roots in trials

observed sections: trials events are made up of observed sections of considerable technical difficulty; a marshal scores each rider

off-road motorcycles: motorcycles designed purely or partly for use off metaled roads

passing line: the fastest line to overtake

pegs: footrests

power slide: using engine power to slide side-on through a turn

power stroke: the piston stroke when the spark plug ignites the fuel

power valve: a valve sited near the exhaust port that alters engine characteristics and increases the power range

racing line: the fastest line around the course

rear disc brake: see **front disc brake**

rev: the number of times an engine turns in a minute

showing a wheel: pushing the front wheel into the range of vision of a rider in front

signaler: an aide who holds up a board to show the rider's position in a race

skid plate: a heavy-duty steel plate to protect the bottom of a trials bike engine from grounding

stages: trials events are often divided into stages, which are subdivided into *observed sections*; this allows the event to visit different areas and tackle different terrain

supercross: a stadium form of motocross

suspension: a system to allow up-and-down movements of the wheels and cushion the bike

swinging arm: the entire rear wheel assembly of a modern off-road bike is mounted on an arm, attached to the main body of the bike, which allows it to pivot up and down

tank slapper: hitting the fuel tank with the arms when the front wheel wobbles

tear-offs: multilayered transparent covers on goggles

throttle: the accelerator, mounted on the handlebars

toolkit: a box of useful tools

torque: power at low revs

trials: an event in which riders are judged on skill and technique over difficult terrain

two-stroke: an engine in which the second stroke of the piston is the *power stroke*

wheelbase: the distance from wheel hub to wheel hub

wheelie: lifting the front wheel

whoops: closely spaced bumps in motocross

Index